Apostrophes

woman at a piano

BY E.D. BLODGETT

BuschekBooks

Canadian Cataloguing in Publication Program

Blodgett, E. D. (Edward Dickinson), 1935-
    Apostrophes: woman at a piano

Poems.
IBN 0-9699904-0-5

    I. Title

PS8553.L56A82 1996   C811'.54   C96-900004-9
PR9199.3.B54A82 1996

Second printing, November 1996   Fourth printing, February 1997
Third printing, December 1996

Other books of poetry by E.D. Blodgett:
    take away the names (1975)
    sounding (1977)
    Beast Gate (1980)
    Arché/Elegies (1983)*
    Musical Offering (1986)*
    Da Capo (1990)
* winner of the Stephan G. Stephannson Poetry Award

Apostrophes: woman at a piano
Printed and bound in Canada by Hignell Printing Limited, Winnipeg, Manitoba
Design: Marie Tappin

BuschekBooks, P.O.Box 74053, 35 Beechwood Avenue
Ottawa, Ontario K1M 2H9
BuschekBooks editor: John Buschek

We cannot bear witness to the sun.

R.F. Taylor

. . . but plainly to propound.

Wallace Stevens

Car si la poésie n'est pas, comme on l'a dit "le réel absolu," elle en est bien la plus proche convoitise et la plus proche appréhension, à cette limite extrême de complicité où le réel dans la poésie semble s'informer lui-même.

St.-John Perse

Tibi

Contents

Woman at a Piano

I wanted to tell you this: a woman, sitting,
her hands almost not her own, sitting through long afternoons,
the light changing as it enters the room, the light,
in perpetual play between her flesh and air within the room —:
I could not tell if it was yellow I saw or yellow's warmth,
but over her skin the light moved, and into the light the warmth
of flesh, and she, the sense of stillness and flesh that disappears,
sitting within the light, music falling from her hands.
I wanted to tell you this and something more — the colour

of the pose, of late afternoon across the sea, the birds
intermittent through the waves. Colours are never single, they
compose each other, green calling to blue, and blue departing, saying
what we rush to hear, running under the trees, across the fields,
begging to hear the final words of blue, touching ourselves where shades
of blue come down, stroking the going away, unable to reply, forgetting the name
of blue, its darkness in our hands. Is this what she wants to say, the woman
in the room, the woman who does not move, sitting forever in the light,
only her hands and face revealed, no fold within her dress, her hands

across the keys touching music, music touching the air, the air
no longer simple with green and blue and yellow, but oh it must dance,
a room of crystal, a room of old chairs, a room of bright flowers, all
crystal no more, nor chair nor flower, nor cool brightness within the fall
of light, but falling from her fingers, falling through the late
air, beyond the doors of glass, across the lawn and into the trees where
birds within the rituals of music begin to rise within the long going away
of blue. The woman sits. I tell you this: I want to open my mouth becoming
blue, becoming the dark, leaning into stillness, touch touching touch.

Flowers

Just soldiers walking past a tomb, heads bent and walking into
rain: how can I rise from the pictures you sent, all scattered
on the floor, gray pictures of something whose end I could not
see, all the streets blocked, pictures of no colour but twilight
and rain? Somewhere I saw a dog sleeping by a wall. You said he was
dead, and where the soldiers walked, the air around them dead, as
soldiers on a frieze, flowers fell where their boots passed, heads curved—:

how small you would have thought the street, its lamps bent, no
light coming down but gray light where all the blossoms lay. No one,
you said, is buried in the tomb but pieces put together to make
a doll of other soldiers' parts. The pieces, you said, never fit.
Why did you say nothing of the women, faces all alike and gray, faces
bent against the ground, their flowers lost beneath the rain? I tell you
where the tomb is laid: within my eyes the soldiers walk, and flowers

and the gray of women passing in the rain. But how to call them,
what names to put upon that shape that huddles there? And why
do birds come to walk against my cheeks, cold fires of hope within
their eyes, gazing at the tracks soldiers leave? I cannot sleep,
I want to ask of women where flowers begin. I start again: why are there
petals falling from my eyes, fountains of slow petals that drift
into birds, becoming what flower again, what soldier, what twilight?

How lakes—lakes of blue music, their waves that echo under
the breaking moon, lakes beneath the cold lashes of rain—how
to recall the patience of water going away? Lakes where the riders
come exploding out of night, their hooves against the shore, the
pain of rocks that split, falling into night: where are they,
the world steeped in the waiting of lakes, huge eyes of no closing,
they stare out against their birthing blue, or darker, succumbing

to the change of fall. And what is within them, the great fish,
the snaking reeds? This is the wound of water against my feet.
Anything that I might say I want to come to one question: how
to become the helplessness of lakes, nothing at all to know, to
be for fish to turn with never a sound within, all weathers to tear
across the skin, and in the end to stop in ice? I shall not ask
why lovers—how many to count—walk there, their feet against the broken

stone, remembering the horses passing, nor why the moon is a stone
that floats within the dark, how small the riders are, going away, their
heads bent, dreaming of lakes. The weather of lakes sits on my hands.
Whatever it says cannot be heard, nor has it weight. It must be what
the holy is. We put it where our faces are—yes, I saw it's what you
did, and you spoke of sacred things, the shade of mountains on your
cheeks. Lakes, you said, are so, a sarabande of sorrow in your eyes.

Song

Or birds: the rain hanging in the leaves, and indistinct,
of colours fading, or that you feel you might become flower, the dirt
seeping over your feet, your arms hovering into green, and even your head,
the sound of rain dimming, eyes no longer able, emptiness and rain
falling within your skull, and birds calling in the rain, the world
becoming soft, the world found, the world barely heard, the sun

put out, the stars all false. I cannot believe the shapes of the moon,
nor consequences of the tides and order of the poles. It is a gravity put
elsewhere: a law for birds, a law for rivers, a law for stones that turn
in space, the light that bends, each its own law. And so beneath the rain
the birds sit, their dampened calls rippling into space, becoming place.
I want to lie upon the grass, the rain entering my flesh, to take the shape

of grass, hearing where the world is, a stone shifting in the frost,
north dissolving. Or birds: Brancusi failed to understand, his bent
bird that stands still in space, the air around it dead. What
begins for birds, and where are the sides of space? This is the praise
of nowhere at all, the sentence that comes within our ken from somewhere else,
sentence of falling suns, exorbitant stars, your eyes becoming rain.

Gift

Allora fu la paura un poco quieta,
che nel lago del cor m'era durata . . .

The silence grew. Nothing came from silence, but trees of silence
put on their leaves of green silence, nor was the moon the moon
but silence echoing the silence of the sun. I could not tell if she,
the woman standing on the lake beneath the moon, if she were silence or
the look of woman standing there. And how she stood, the dress of
damask descending to her feet, her feet barely carressing the
water still as untouched air beneath, casting the moon into air. This

is where silence speaks, I saw, the woman's shape upon the surface of
the lake gazing at herself, the silence of woman and her form the form
of thought emerging from the water into air, unbroken passage of light falling
and rising into itself. Oh cosmos! The shape of silence must go round and
round, it is the moving into light of tree, of moon, of lake
and woman. Why do I sit upon the shore, and why, lips apart, does
nothing but silence descend into my ears, no words but words become

the silence of themselves? What comes before this place? I think that here
God is mute, absolute and not yet, or but a passage through the air
without a ripple showing there upon the lake, no soughing in the
trees. I am alone with God. We want light, light overflowing. Oh she is
not silence become woman there, she is a fountain that sheds the light
of silence streaming from her face. I cannot think of what
music is, or anything that might come after this, saying how it is.

"*Die Rose ist ohne warum*"

Roses are blind. They open beneath the sun, opening of red, mortality
and love beneath the sun. The silence of roses enters my eyes, opening
them slowly, mortality taking root, ineffable burden of roses wherever
I look. Do roses sleep? Somewhere, I think, roses lie down in dark, unseen,
knees bent like us, arms gone slack, helpless under cover of night. And
roses must dream, unbearable red dreams of suns falling, a universe of

falling suns and fountained skies. Roses must dream, a dream of where
roses come from, dreams of roses that fall from where the air is still
between the sun and moon, cosmos unfulfilled and strewn with auras of
the rose. These must be dreams of blood, and somewhere roses must dream of us
all asleep and our falling between the sun and moon. Rain falls from the same
place, auroraed ground of roses. Was that summer, to stand with arms open

beneath the sky, the rain pouring down upon my flesh, eyes spilling over with
a dream of roses, the sun and moon gone? Who would believe the sky was
mortal too, and roses on the ground? To see them open, the folds of their
mouth yearning for the rain: this is how blindness comes—first from the sun, then
rain, the roses standing in your eyes, the light gone, and silence
broken, petals falling—one and then another into dark, filling the air.

*L*ate Fall

Why do they, the floes of ice in late fall, why do they strike so
against the other, the river sealing up? And what to say of that hollow
o not music, but remnants drifting in the air? Not music but its silence
falling. Here is where space is found, discharging inner bits of sound,
unheard, inviolate, fragmentary shaping of the air. I could not stop, but
moved to place my hands there, believing that hands, the dust of ageing

sifting from them, might be as hands forever in the silence there. But what
is this believing—of silence, ice, and rivers in their ending? And what do you
believe, no hand able to reach the quick of silence, purities I thought
the air concealed, standing at the edge of water becoming whiter element?
The sound of rivers in their mortalities—: *that* was to hear, and roses in
their awful absence. I beg you, the silence falling past my hands, hold

back the snow, ashen petals of the rose unfolding out of emptiness,
dissolution of roses within the slower flowing of late rivers. Why have I
left my hands there, nothing for them to do? At heart this sound has no
innocence to reply: it is absence where it starts, gnawing at the sides
of bones, the wind within them to the marrow. The whiteness of the air
flakes—no, the air falls, flowing from bones, our bones, the rose undone.

Nowhere falls the rain but in us.
It falls from where silence is, falling away, into dark. The shade
is veiled in rain, and night—what colours!—dripping from
the rain, the wet of blue against your face. Silence is
rain, transient within the air, our breath, inhalation
of night, blue falling away. Rain broods, it crouches in our bones,
remembering the moon, other silences, stars.

*B*efore Departing

When flowers first broke from my hand, they did not seek the sun,
nor did they wish to eat the air and light, but when they came it was
how flowers come upon a fallen house, pushing the smaller stones down
until the ground frays, feeding on the bones, white flowers, flowers
that had no time for tears, bones thinning into dust, cold sprays of
dust—: I thought it was the winter with flowers standing under snow.

B^{irth}

When tears come, they do not come as water in the eyes, they come
as children you have lost, beautiful faces of tears falling past
into lives that you shall never know. You want to call upon the stars,
to bid them gaze upon them, filling them with light, faces of children
upon your cheeks slipping away. How could it be that tears have lives,
seeking mothers, seeking consolations of the dark—tears
that lie in pieces in every room you move within? Tears are not
what we wanted to say, they are the children for whom we had no words.

Dying

When my father died, you bore within your hand nothing,
nothing and daffodils. Your hand was white, and they were so
yellow spilling over nothing where they rose. I wept
within my eyes. When you lay dead, I was away, alone and
falling through a cold country, nothing familiar within
my eyes. Did someone remember daffodils were once

within your hands, nothing changing shape? And so I failed
to carry flowers to your death, bringing nothing in the end.
Who shall, I wanted to ask, offer flowers to the death
of flowers, bearing them through that cold country, saying
nothing? When, then, did we speak, not speaking words, but
speaking daffodils, eternities that turn within our blood?

My Father, Sitting

And I remember you within the garden, roses in the air
and bees burning within the folds of their mouths. You sat
upon a bench of stone, the green shawl of shade falling over
your back. Your silence is one with roses. A cat lies within
your hands. I cannot tell whether it is the cat I see or hands
stroking through the shade. Have you become Chinese or the look

of death, your eyes turning toward your soul where roses ease their roots
unseen, without a sound? You are cosmos and what it means. Our stars
are of no use, nor sun and rain. Nothing moves but bees, and they
are lost in light. You cannot feel roses—only roses feel, the stony
soil of your breath, its slower returns, infinitesimal springs
coming back invisible with bees, the smell of roses remembered.

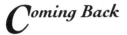# Coming Back

Already the lilacs have flowered. Sitting on the grass, I have
nothing left to do. How have I become testament, my
body but a page, the sun unchanged, lying in the green
grass? The last time I walked here, you carried lilacs
in your hand. I could not see your eyes, already turning

upon themselves. I think the sun shines for the moon alone, gazing
into death. I could not touch the flowers in your hand, passing
toward their death in water, the air drenched with the odour
of lilacs, my body become the flowering of lilacs in your hand. We turn
blank beneath the sun, unknown how much the moon's kin we are.

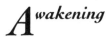Awakening

Florence, you said—the golden, final summer when you were
young, the light burning in your hair beneath the sky, and cries
of mockingbirds that rang among the leaves, their one song
the song of summer entering the air until the air, you said, began
to sing. I cannot recall the songs, so sudden was their change, but how
in freshets ecstasy came down into the afternoon. Once

I opened my eyes to see the sun within your mouth, the silence of
your smile that spread slowly over the earth. We sit still
within the golden rain transformed. I see there were no
finalities, the birds assuming silence for their song. Flowers rise
unheard within the air, and grass, wherever your face looks
down, intent upon perpetual deliverances of green.

Berceuse

The light has changed—: it was
a moment when the birds came down to feed upon the ground.
Suppose you cradled music in your hand, nocturnal airs
through which the moon moved without care, the stars rising
around your head? I think you would be bound to dance, you
and all the birds across the fields turning in celestial rounds, the trees
upon the margins bending darkly in the air. Not music,

you said, but light that parts opacities of flesh, unable after
to see the line between the envelope of skin and air once
ambient, flowing through what once were hands. Nor are there lines,
I heard you say, in nature, nothing but the play of light upon
a ground of yellow, blue and red, substance refracted, nothing
becoming tree, nothing beyond the light dancing on your
skin, and hands that open crepuscular air, the moon a flower.

efrain

I thought you were dead, the last tear shed, images
of daffodils finally laid to rest, and what remains of you
settled within the earth. I have no desire, the great sleep
of earth entering my bones. I cannot bear the sorrow of
daffodils, their stems cut and laid upon the ground. I thought

you were dead, startled gazing into ponds to see not mine, but your
face returned to me, your eyes, the shades of bafflement that once crossed
your brow, the light shaken from the sky. To whom does my flesh belong
and, speaking your name, is it into earth, pools of tranquil
surfaces, that I must look, to know how your reply would be? I thought

you were dead, the light strewn upon the ground—no, flowers passing, the dark
rising into air. My mother must be this silence, the earth at last
entering the earth. I cannot speak and, opening my mouth, it is
flowers I could not hold within my hands that exhale before
my eyes, the last light upon my lips, the earth returning daffodils.

Now your face is old, its edges steeped in twilight. Nothing is more alone than that light. It sits against a shore, small heaps of wood beside its feet, waves that fall outside of sound, the wind itself worn. The words you speak no longer seem yours, each taking shapes of what you say unseen, morphologies without the change of death

within the air. I can never recall the sea without your presence somewhere near, nor is there knowing where wood that washes up comes from, nor wind, nor waves. This is what we are—aspects of the air. Sometimes I think that I shall never wake. I dream the words you spoke. I hear the earth breathe, your breath, and wind falls.

I had forgotten the smell of pines, the heavy smell that sinks
within the chest, of pines that stood among the rocks beside
the sea, the sun slashed by needles and the dark falling before
us on the shore. In that place, growing dark, we stood. I cannot
recall your face, nor mine, intent upon that white remembered sea,
breathing the shared odour of pines, the far boats transparent
in the sun. Hermes, you said, must be walking somewhere near, stirring

the pines within the dark. Your words are afraid within my hands
when night comes, everything falling against the earth, nor can I
bear your Hermes there, the sleep he brings and death, filling
my eyes with pines against a burning sea. A wind I did not know
blows within my bones—or I am that wind, a chill passage on
the sea, tearing the dark of root and rock? When it rains, my friend,
the rain is theirs, the tears mine, falling through your words.

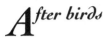 After birds

The birds at sunset always move slowly into the west, drawn
into the sun, the white of their bodies becoming blue, dispersing, sun-
set of birds —: no echo, the light, the trees, the disappearance of
the birds all departing within your eyes. I cannot look. It is the silence
of your eyes that settles into mine I turn from, sudden flight

of birds between us, nothing to touch, edging closer into the light
until the birds are gone. The sunlight I recall is always grave where
ever you are. Why, remembering the light, do deaths of small children
enter there, nothing in their eyes, extinguished stars, something of
sound that never reaches us falling through the light, each one alone?

Your eyes are roses in the dark. The night lies upon my hands,
the folds of darkness falling through my fingers. Where
to walk, and where is the earth turning somewhere beneath
my feet, and gardens of roses, their roots that draw the
dark into themselves? I fear petals falling, fragrant autumns

of roses passing over my face, the dust in my hands, the night
unfolding from your eyes. What's to be done with dust, the stars
settled? The rain does not reach the dark, the sun turns
helpless in the air. Within my hands space cradles
infinities of roses, the fallen look of dark.

*A*utumnal Air

The memory of music is a tree that comes suddenly out of air, and you
would point, and there beyond you fingers, under the sun, it was, one
leaf after another appearing on its boughs, the ground where the light
shone through scattered with shade. This was summer, the fullness of
the tree, and then fall, the green gone, the trees absorbing the last
of the sun, each leaf at random drawn back within the air, forgetting —
then silence, then the tree gone. All summer beneath the tree we lay, growing

old, memories for ourselves, and gazing on the shadows that played over
our flesh. What is it, to touch shade, to dance within the light, flesh
knowing flesh? Sometimes we looked and saw it was an echo, the light
that fell there, and we, beneath the sun, the tree, and darkly passing
shade, we lived, our flesh reflecting light, the dust of late summer
rising from us into the sun. Recalling is a dying gesture, cadences of hands
that keep the sun's time, hands stroking silence, and nothing more.

Winter enters your body—the light first, and then
memories of it. The light is one with dying gods, the dust
amid the fallen corn, shadows of crows descending into
afternoons. Music does not avail, nor flowers. How many years
I wanted to touch your hand before the light diffused
within your flesh, to take winter and the death

of gods away. It is not gods who die, but us, no light
that falls from spent eyes, nor are the crows more
than crows, moving up and down the earth. But somewhere you are,
transparent beneath the sky, the light of winter entering
my eyes. How could the gods have been when we are they
who are the light, and memories of winter, the parting shades?

When roses open, music hangs suspended in the air, enchanted
rain that never reaches ground. I want to move my hand, but nothing
near my hand stirs, the air without life against my flesh, nothing but
roses opening unseen. Perhaps you were always young. Who can say
what empires mean, ages gazing on the sea expanding into air,
no one growing old but passing slowly into the sea, becoming one
horizon, no one remembering, empires of voices fading into

evening air? O roses! I thought that this was where beginning was,
overture and fragrance in the air, eyes that utter silence against
the dying of the day. Gazing into the roses of your eyes, I cannot
see but opening within—perhaps the sea that lies infinitesimal
there, and blue. The children of eternity are roses alone, roses
rising in your eyes. No one owns the rain. It falls where roses
are, the endless twilights of your eyes, horizons giving way.

Mine is a family of sad faces. No one remembers why. Perhaps it was
the rain of that country—gray, interminable rain that fell for years
through the air, a country of ancient willows that sweep the surfaces
of rivers, slowly. The windows of our houses were high, the curtains
heavy, water beading on the glass. The stories in the long winters were
always the same—: no one was allowed to die, standing beside
the slow rivers, staring at water passing. I carry the words of those

stories in my hands, muffled words distilling now and then within
the air. I think a willow grows within my chest, the tendrils of
its branches always seeking rivers. I have never seen the sun, and
no one ever spoke of what it was, nor did they speak of how the days began
or who our Eve and Adam may have been. Birds there are in that
country huddling in the rain. You would not believe their songs of stone
transmuted, and light, music itself becoming gray, wearing away.

A Requiem

All day the sun began to set. It fell slowly, a rain among
autumnal leaves, falling upon a lake, and falling into
your eyes. The dawn was mortal, you said, and everything
it touches dies. The mystery of summer has passed us by,
and memories of other suns upon your face. We gaze into the air,
the look from our eyes floating over the lake, somewhere

trailing off among the trees. The birds have gone already, was all
you wanted to say, and the sound of the words hovered in the air
as ghosts of birds might. This is what the haunted is, flesh
growing old, an emptiness of birds inside our skin. If I should see
your eyes again, the sun would have horizon there, extinguished in
its fall. The dark, my friend, is a gift. No one takes it away.

Weathers

I do not recall when the sun went down, lying beside you in
the dark, eyes closed, your body without life, and if
I slept or dreamt. We are not flesh but weathers of
mortality, early freshets, a fading in the air, a light
that never reaches earth. Birds pass through us, seeking
dust and repose. When the moon entered the room, I did not

see it, but knew it on my skin, feeling night envelope us.
What mortality is this, to touch your face and stroke
the moon in passing there, night and flesh within my grasp? No one
knows if we will wake, and where that waking is. The wind
enters my breath, bearing the rain, fragrances of roses
into my body, and summer, and colours of lakes when the light

of day recedes, something calling in the leaves unseen. Thus
the merest breath is ritual we do not know, transfiguring
the air. Lying beside you underneath the moon and waiting for
your eyes to open in the dark, I see they are no longer eyes,
and we are gardens, nothing in the air to hear but flowers
blown beneath the moon, a wake of petals floating through the dark.

Dreams are roses, their roots beneath the ground, the opening
of each flower wounding the air, and when we sleep, their odour
is our breath. How could it be I dreamt of you again, your eyes,
the music of your voice that falls in airs of roses, entering
my flesh once more? No light within dreams that does not fall
from where the moon turns within the sky. I think now that I too

have died, to see you standing there, the moon falling over your
face, and one rose rising in your hand, its stem cut, beginning now
to die. I cannot take it from your hand, gazing into the ground
of your eyes to see the death of roses there. Dreams, my friend,
are mortal, the music that we breathe is flesh, and we the air
where moons within the cosmos pass. Roses, then, do not die, they

are, at last, us — to be beneath the sky wherever you are, turning
alone, becoming moon. When we sleep, roses leap within our flesh,
no one remembering who we were, whose eyes opened into air, whose voices
through the gardens fell. This is my rose, offered to you
wherever you may be, rose of my mortality, my breath exhaling
the moon, giving itself up. Nothing that it says is mine.

*A*ntiphonal

Children never danced within your eyes, but birds found there
old reveries of departure—ships, horizons and remains of sacrifice
left upon the shore—birds that never uttered sounds that I
could hear, birds entranced, waiting beneath the moon, and all flesh
consumed. Evenings are not oracular, but where the sun, turning
into solitude, descends, the words that you spoke falling from a dream

of birds and into night. No one saw your face, nor were they words
that spilled from your mouth, but distances that drift among stars,
a long gaze of gods. The one dance I saw was what mortality had made,
a figure floating beneath the moon. We are nocturnal airs, our music
the moon, remembering the sun and transience of birds. Of this music we
are breath, a giving in to air, a passage of the moon gone from sight.

E*os*

The sun rises over the rose of your body, shades withdrawing and
the light from your eyes entering the air, the sun exhaled. We were
not born, as other roses are, to fill the air, our roots within
the dark, nor to depart at some season's end, bearing the burdens of
our flesh within our hands. When we breathe, we are translucencies
of air, our bones left to earth, the earth reflecting shadows of ourselves —

the grass, the rose, the fallen leaf. All we are of earth is
the going round, our dancing light within the air. Speaking now
so to you is my becoming rose, taking the one sun that is within
my mouth, turning to word within the dark, then to bright reveilles of
the air revealed —: so the sun rose, dreams of flesh inflections on
the grass, the first light the breath of eschatologies within your eyes.

R^{ites}

There was no sound within the air, all the bells mute, no one
to give absence shape. When you left, you entered that abyss
where no birds sing. If there are lakes, the lakes are black.
But somewhere held in summer's arms, lovers lie embraced, eyes
bursting with tears that are roses in the sun. They speak of zeniths,
the one sun that lovers see, Aztec in their ecstasy, and nothing
in their words that brings you back, nor winter, nor the bells they did
not hear, the air they see gashed with colours passing, an air

of yellow, blue and red beneath the sun, all breaths of air become
primary in their fall. Summer is no season, its origin the heart
lying open beneath the sun, the brevity of flowers in their eyes
embracing the one sun that lovers own, and every bird calling
and calling their one song within the air they breathe. The mouths
of lovers are an offering, credos to the sun, the dark descending
under the brilliance of their gaze—concealing you, the silence of
the sun, and old Agamemnon's last o moi sundering the air.

*O*blation

The sun lay polyphonic on the ground. The grass sang its thin
green song, and somewhere roses uttered rose. It was of music
unable to raise its hands, of music that could not find finality,
of music where the din dissolves, the music of nothing outside
but music's desire unfolding into air. The apple trees blow
their memories of snow, and transience, nostalgias all white.
Holding this flower, the sun enters my hands, a flower wholly of

the sun and transmutations of the sun. So we are the sun's fruit
suspended from a cosmic air, no one to hear the languid rubati
of the wind among the trees that we compose. On certain afternoons
the lakes that drift around themselves take the whole sky in—:
the stars, the sun, the moon, and blue unfathomable within. We are
the shores, pears that hang scored upon that blue where aspects of
the sun float and echoes of ourselves, no farther than the stars.

C

Snow, you said. I believe in snow. Some believe in rivers, the flowing
beneath the sun, and others the same bird within the same tree,
everyone glimpsing themselves passing through the shade. But lovers,
open to the moon, sleep upon the grassy floors of the world,
the sleep where they are held their one belief, a sleep that falls
upon them as rose petals fall, a snow of petals rising from the south,
seasons of the snow that bear fragrances of spring within the turning

of their breaths, and deep within the endless falling of their sleep,
oh hear them, they sing their new song, their breath filling with
ambrosial odours of God! Their prelude was to say *rejoice*, their text
the falling rose steeping sleep. The cosmos, then, sleeps, the shape
of its sleeping round, the sun and moon in one another's arms, and dreams
that lovers dream flowering the air. The light they breathe does not
begin, nor newness streaming the air, nor affirmations of the rose.

I cannot imagine you have died. I look upon the ground—:
it is the ground I see, nothing more. Or flowers, or
simplicities of leaves. Sometimes I think of where you were
and I, and think then of finding somewhere there, walking through
the same slow rain, stopping at each place—this tree and rock,
that surprise among the leaves—to see them in their nakedness, but trees,
placing my hand upon an essence of the ground, a kind of chaos

foresworn. Perhaps the sun is timeless now, an old sun that's grown
eternal from the fire, ignescent purities descending through
the emptied air, only what it is left. Look: the sun lies upon
the ground, and we upon the sun becoming one. Now to imagine
you have died, the sun entering the ground. So the absolute
begins, a darkness grown transparent beneath the sun. Show me
your breath, its shape of late leaves turning white within the air.

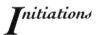Initiations

I woke desiring rain. I cannot touch the sky, nor planets in
their course, and distances that drift through the mind—other
immortalities. But once returning through rain, no longer able
to see, I felt the stones lying everywhere against the ground.
What other finitudes am I to offer you but these small stones,
being only what they are, and infinite wearing away? It is a gift
of wholly giving up, motionless beneath the rain, remembrance

anywhere. And so I sat within the fall of rain, the knowing of rain
running down my flesh, slipping away. How to tell you then I saw
the season on your face—the rain, the weathers of humility, and music
of birds muffled in the rain, the pity of it sitting in my bones? Were I
to touch your face, roses would have stood within your eyes, their slow
unfoldings rising toward the rain, their roots beneath us, among stones,
and morning in its bright similitudes breaking through the rain.

Birds before departing turn above the wood, descents in long arcs
traced against the fallen fields, old trees their dreams bent
with fruit, threads of birds that gather among the destinies of air.
How will I recall the numbers of birds circling within my eyes, and where
we played beneath them, invisible calligraphies within the light,
and your walking through the fields, the sun flowing down your back?
I might have touched you then —: a cosmos would have entered my body, hands
overcome with galaxies, the meaning of the moon upon my skin, mortality

falling from me to lie upon the fields, an old shirt waiting in the wind
for winter. When, now, does absence in its spell begin? Is it autumn
flowering, each time the last, under the sun? I fear forgetting, words
that fray within the wind, a track lost, the dark that drifts into
the earth, the dreams of old trees, unravelling. This far alone are we brought
and birds in their diasporas, skin without the moon for light, to gaze
upon the sun in its conclusions, auguries we cannot read blowing
through us, naked, words the sun speaks, nothing audible but light.

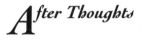

After Thoughts

I saw the sun within your eyes, a small cosmos burning there,
and other stars, other moon, and certain birds that sit within
the mind, breathing weathers, and where your gaze descends upon
the ground, grass appears, flowers and stones, the rain prismatic
in the air. Absolutes repose upon your hands, and where you walk
within that light, touches of music graze your skin. The world

cannot grow old, turning upon its dream of eschatology and final
fires. No more to do than place my hand upon the grass, to see
green where my fingers were, hands full of grace, and leave
immortality upon the ground, seeing the sun rise within your eyes —:
this is deathless wish enough, and all prayer, all desire is the grass
replying to your gaze, and flowers, stones, and cadences of rain.

#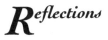

You sat within the window, light falling in patches on your face,
sunlight a crown upon your hair. Can the sun descend so
through blue vacuities of air, the clouds, among leaves to form
an afternoon upon your skin, and nothing in the afternoon
but what remains of you in light and shade? Touching you now, I could
not feel more than what might move within the wind, a shade that deepens
under the falling sun, cast upon the glass. Where will you be, the sun

gone from sight, the glass untouched against the air? We live within
the air, the light, the shade, the turns of thought that afternoons
may take, no more than flowers—naked, alone, and passing from
sight. Your hands within the light have nothing left to do but hold
fragility, a radiance returned. If being moved, it would be seen
a circle in the air, a dance that turns inside out, inciting
the sun, the flesh and leaf of afternoons translucent in the glass.

esper

Sitting beside you in the twilight, your face half turning into
night, I saw it was a lunar pool where leaves of words that we
had spoken slip beneath the wind into horizons of the moon
and water. Final phases are rarely full—: even the moon slows,
its crescents going out. Does it remember then its great grandeur,
radiant through summer nights, its open-eyed stare of lovers

lying by the lakes, distance falling through the light, the lovers
phototropic in their ecstasies, lakes flooding, and fish become
falling stars? Or only its late autumns, branches of the cracking
trees across its face, its fragments hanging in the sky? So we live
within the moon, the moon in us, my friend. To go on talking, our words
drifting past, is lunatic, each one etching the dark to make it stay.

hards

In the end, the sun comes apart. It was a wound, you thought, the air
opening within, and memories of other suns unmoved in their
finalities, spread out at last upon the ground, the gilded trees
a fault within the sky, birds become stars, but brightest at
the end, the sun comes apart, a sound of crystal struck once,
memories of other suns, echoes on a ground—: not, then, epiphany
that takes note, nor in its consummation Aztec. Nothing comes beyond the sun

but you, among the shades of that concluded day, bent upon the sun,
gathering within your hands what it had been. Forever is no more
than this, to sit within the dark, to see you arched in solitude,
the harvest of your hands untouched within the air. Sorrow does not
grow, it is to breathe the air where one irrevocable sun has passed,
our flesh the place where it went out, solace of a galaxy. What
words for summoning the moon, turning cold within our mouths?

# Entrances

You slept, the light from the moon rising from your face. I thought
it was the moon that slept, the light withdrawing under clouds,
cadences of music breathing near you unseen. It was a season
entering the room, season of tentative departures, squalls of birds
and their return. Why do I see you always by the sea, sleeping along
the shore, the play of water under the moon moving against the shape
your body makes, endless exhalations of the sea upon the shore? When we

sleep, how do they take shape within—the sea that breathes, the wind
of birds, the moon dreaming moon? And where, at last, does it find room
to dwell, the earth entering the air? I remember willows near
the shore, refusing longest to lose their final leaves, until they all
have fallen through the air, turning back to earth, their music closing
beneath the moon, willows within their darkling sleep. Nothing else
to recall: your sleep is my breathing here, the moon arisen in my mouth.

Even the ground exhaled the light. It is not grass, you might
have said, we walk upon, but fresh nostalgias of green, as if the gods
recalled how once the world appeared beneath the first rising of
the sun. Look now upon the birds: no song fills the air—it is
the air that breathes in long arpeggios, the air flowing over
from their mouths and entering your eyes. No nearer can
we come to some divinity than this translation of the sun

bearing witness over us. I might stumble now upon
you sleeping on the ground, and flowers with your eyes
would open, music leaping from them. Is it possible to place
my hands among those flowers flowing in the light, the memories
of roses rising? I cannot be the sun, but you, where birds within
the overtures of evening pass, you are where the moon respires
in your gaze, unearthed, the opening of flowers in my hands.

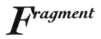ragment

I never saw your hands before. Beside you, fallen into
solitudes, they lay, unmoved, intent upon a passage of
the sun, and trees came up about them, abiding in their
seasons, leaves within the light translucent in their fall.
Whenever birds sing, fragilities of light spread out upon
your hands, a wound within the sky resounding through the
trees. Mortality in heaven's mouth would run among the smallest

leaves, summoning the sun, music to irradiate the air.
I never saw your hands, but as I see them now, asleep within
the passing of the sun, the slow descent of leaves, I think
that they will never wake, a fallen sun upon them. No song
could be more alone—a cosmos, then, of one song, the sound
beyond the sun expired. One cosmos holds your hands—:
leaves passing, consummations of the sun, a piece of air.

A nnunciation

A bird sang within my ear. No one beheld how heaven came
and bent around it. A tree stood up within the quick of spring,
the merest breath of roses settled in my flesh, the sphere
of the sun suspended over us. Where you walk now beneath
the tree, the music of your moving can possess no echo known.
Do not ask, as spring enters me, if any epilogue

can be, or if, the soonest moment after, I, except in some
similitude might pass, and with me bird and heaven, roses, tree
and spring, consumed by silence. Where is spring, music gone,
the passage of your walking but the air? Let me call your name
of one ecstatic aria, becoming bird within your ear, syllables
descending from their skies, the o of roses turning in your flesh.

There is no rose that burst upon a summer's day that ever rose
so within the garden of your eyes. The stillness after lay
heavily upon my hands, and bees within the day began to disappear,
inhaled in sudden ecstasies. It cannot be that I have flesh,
but moving now my hands within the stillness, what will they feel
but leavings of the light, a dawn in analogue that hovers in
your eyes. What name is there for seasons where we live, the light

that enters me so that rising suns and their similitudes
come forth wherever bees and roses are? No one discerns that roses
opening and eyes have any difference—: it is a season when hypothesis
cannot be shaped. I walk within the garden of your eyes, the rose
of your sun rising on whatever I might be, its fragrance
forming stars and moon, trees and grass and air. This is our
immortality, a rose unnamed, the knowing in our breath.

R^{ain}

The air around your body sleeps. If the rain should fall there,
who would there be, anywhere within the world, to carry it
away? Is it, then, the year going out within your breath,
exhalings of the leaf, or you becoming air, filling with
itself and rain, translucency asleep, where each of us shall pass,
one by one? Somewhere solitude lies down, uncovered and

asleep, the iambs of its breathing emptying, a universe
assuming shape—: stars first and then the sun, planets and
the wind, the grass upon the ground wherever you may be.
Breathing your sleep, a solar air enters me, the light
of other stars. If divinity were mind, where within
the universe would it be sleeping, its breathing being what it is?

oons

Your eyes entered mine. I want the name of darkness now
to tell you that the green we see when we behold the grass,
the blue against the sky, to tell you this is dream. The sun
does not go burning through the heavens, nor is the moon alone —:
it sleeps upon the grass, floating at your feet. But where is there
an entrance into dark, your eyes gazing into me, the light

eclipsing light? The moon, then, that floats within your eyes must in
its phases slowly enter mine till we become all moon
and turn tidal there, and breathing through our eyes a universe
of light. The rest is dark, opacity of where we pass. We live
within the grass, the blue we thought the sky was. Let me touch
the grass, it will appear a glove around my hand, adrift in dark.

A^{*ria*}

Music rises from the night, the ground beneath your feet
sighing where you pass. Were there birds within that night,
they would have stayed their song, the night air enough,
floating past their eyes. This is music of the merest
things —: of stones and wood and fallen pieces of the earth.
We cannot get away from this, you and I, this music in
absentia, this utter innerness. What if I should hold within

my hands your bones in all their purity? And where to let
them be at night beneath the muted birds, their eyes
burning in the moon, everything become air? I must have gone
within the ground to follow you, to see the stones within
their dissolutions so. Mortality must sound so
departing from the bone, an air within another room, and you
within the air, the night exhaling from your eyes.

Eternity adrift within your eyes —: it is the wind that passes
round the planets, asking, where am I, and other winds replying
in the dark whatever winds reply. I want to take it in my hands,
eternity or wind, the breath that planets in their turn exhale,
to lay it tranquil at your feet, becoming air that you might draw
it in, a breath in time, the darkness of eternity, the measured
inhalations entering the darkness of your body, breath forever

growing in the dark. What is eternity, to see it in
your eyes, immortal red of roses, the wear of stones against
your hand's flesh, assurances of sunlight in the night, the moon,
then, coming, going, breathing light, analogies of evening
everywhere within the patience of the grass? What eternity is there
to take? We sit within eyes unspeaking, their gazing given
to them, and passages that echo farther than the turning of sun.

No one would have thought that it was you, standing there beneath
the tree, your face veiled in rain. It must have been a dream,
our breath escaping whitely into dream. You never said a word,
nor I, but harkened only to the rain falling from the leaves
upon the ground. There is no rain that falls that does not fall
within the ear, recalling other afternoons of rain and other
solitudes, and looking into rain, I saw the barest shape your face

put on, and saw within your gaze the one bird that sang, its song
distilling into rain. There is no rain that falls outside of time,
and yet it is a thing forever bringing other rains to mind. Perhaps
the memory is rain, falling softly somewhere in us, and you, the song
that rose alone within your eye—: I cannot say that this is dream,
the whiteness of it entering the rain. There must be rains that never
end, my friend, a rain that in its being falls, possessing solitudes.

The wind was blowing through your hair. Tell me, why do flowers
stand up there, unsown and rootless in the sun? And when you speak,
birds in alphabet appear, the coming of their song unseen
upon your breath. Music is only inhaled—not song, nothing that
your tongue has shaped, but something in the ear that settles in the flesh
and finally in our bones. How is it possible to see the wind

scored, and birds inscriptions in the air? Sometimes speaking so
to you, I see you are a tree, your flowers standing in my eyes, a dawn
where birds in their enchantments hang. Not one of any word that floats
upon my breath is mine. How to speak of birds unmoved, arboreal
splendours of the sun? Invocations, invocations and no more—: entrance
of voice into flesh, a breath of flowers cast into my eyes.

ullabies

Between the fall of flowers and the light, I woke, inhaling night
and gravities of stars, to find you gone. I called your name against
the dark, syllables spilling from my mouth across the floor. Should
I stumble on you in the dark, what can I say to call you from
your nameless sleep? It must be stars that I inhale, mythologies
of names that fill my flesh. But what is there to know of stars, Orfeo's

bright fall? Or you, the fable of your name shredded now
beneath the wind? No illumination in the stars, no cosmos but
the flesh, their white silence cast within our bones. Where, then, is
the sun but somewhere going down within the air we breathe, light
within our mouths? How to name flowers, abandoned in the night, or name
ourselves, stripped from frost, momentary spells the sun displays?

Coming out of dream, my hand grazed your face, unsure of where
it was. You did not speak, silence growing in the night larger
than the moon. My fingers held your face, to know you in the dark,
your flesh within its silence, frail bones beneath. We could not move,
the dark spread upon us, coming out of dream. No rose I took
within my hands with that temerity, fearful of fragilities,

the shape of your mortality opened there. The moon could have
no greater gravity, oceans unfolding in their dark, the shores
in bloom. I felt the night entering my hands, planets and
the moon disclosed. This is where we are, lying open in
our dark, tendrils of silence alive within our bones, coming out
of dream, hands taking root, possessed of your becoming rose.

*M*oon Flower

The music in the air was music that had flowered from beneath
a sea in summer's plenitude to settle on the grass. It stood
by moments, green and talismanic, moments of a music, moon
and turning stars within its summoning, majesty of music
that is music of the flesh alive and radiant within
the rising of the sea, and where you stood, it was the standing forth
of music, trees within their silence bending toward the sound, and birds

amazed at random in the air above the sea, the light that in
its flowing rose from you invisible, its opening into
the air an incantation of the sea returning. Music is flesh,
possessing in its turning immortality, the longing of
the trees in their humility, the stars not stars but where you are
within the night. The universe is not the sun, it is of you,
uttering the moon, no other moon ascending in the air.

Taking Note

It's Sunday here. Across the world I see you in your winter still
lying in sleep, and here the spring is almost in its fullness
now. The trees within the parks linger in their solitudes,
the flowers on their branches barely open, uncertain in
the air, and were you here, we'd say it was a music, this
unthinking filling in of space, music in its silence seeking

each initial note it is to make, to know and not to know
where it begins. Is this to be within your sleep, to lie
within another's wakeful eyes, music held within a stay
of time, abandoned somewhere to the earth? How helpless are
the flowers here, their being given up to rain and sun, the play
of bees within their momentary folds, their fall prismatic

into summer. You are asleep, an air of spring about to enter you,
and rain, and bees within their early ecstasies, your being
in flower. Music is without beginnings, spring and suns that come
across the earth, the flowers in their passing, summer in
its wakes—: we are both of us asleep, the silences of flowers
filling us, the ground where music in its absence falls.

*B*earing Witness

Your breath takes the night in, your body steeped with stars.
If I were with you now, the rhythm of your breathing in my ears,
the changing moon would spill its light more slowly on my skin, and if
there were a rain falling through your night, its breath and not the rain
would drift into your flesh. No flower breathes so, the air
the rain sheds, other moons going round within its mouth, but this

rose, that your being in my eyes becomes, opening
within the night, the stars, the moon in metamorphosis,
flower there. I cannot speak of blindness now, so seen
through, but what to name the world, memories of rain,
other springs? Nor are you rose, its petals seeking autumns that
I knew, but emanations of the light, reflecting the new moon.

Last Things

Let me speak of simplest things, assurances of tables, the space
they make. Let me remember hands, yours perhaps, at rest upon
the wood of such old tables, and something in the wood that enters in
your hands. If there were time, time would be a table, the endless knowing
of wood possessing us, trees, the wind that they have breathed, and rain,
the seasons of the sun. Thus I bid you, friend, ask nothing else

of me. To speak of what we know is not within us. Words fall
forever from our mouths, a rain of ancient music flowing through
our bones. Sometimes in early winter evenings the young moon comes
briefly into sight. The light over the snow is shadowed, and what
we breathe is what the moon gives. The silence that it sheds becomes
imperative. Its disappearance is possession. Nothing else endures.

*D*ancing

Do not ask of me that I should speak now of the moon, nor of
memory's rose that fades forever at summer's end. No word
would find it where it is—the moon within its ageing—light as it
descends across your sleeping face, entering the dark that turns
around us where we lie. Nor of the moon ending, fluctuations of
eternities adrift within your eyes a final time, the moon
in autumn, petals falling on the earth in fine snow. I want

the silence it contains, to be the moon in flower, a phasing of
the sun in its unfolding, placing silence in your hands, and as
it fades. Beauty is adverbial, never what it is,
you, then, and I become reflections of the late moon,
aspects more distant of the sun, and when we are, our being is
a turn in time. This shape of silence would I offer you, the sun's
rose fallen asleep within your eyes, autumn in the air.

Vigil

I sit beside your bed, watching the shapes of suns going down
across your face. The flowers in the room are dying, and when I touch
your hand, I cannot feel your flesh, but its death alone, the air
of your exhaling carrying your dying everywhere —: a new
moon and sun and stars. Against the sun, crows at random sit,
black, unmoving, roses falling at their feet. The wind is dead,
the sky without a cloud. Theatre, silence, epilogue, and words

taking other words away. But what does death, your dying
now remove? Death fills, my friend, and so reflection is
replaced, simplicities of other suns, cosmos of what we might
have said, an image of air. None of this is ours now. Your dying
shapes my hands, and looking on them now, they are not mine I see,
nor yours, but something like the stones within the ground, unknowing,
earth, silence and the dark coming down, the light gone.

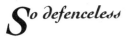

So defenceless

So defenceless in your sleep you lie, the ripened moon at rest
within your flesh. Summer is a rose, nothing departing but
the wind, and in the wind, summer, rose and moon. You thought that when
the summer wind arose, the air rang red. How naked then
the air, its music taking root. What would I touch, my hand
upon your back, mortalities the moon makes, breathing through

the summer air, flowers blowing somewhere in the dark, the wind
departing through the grass? Nothing seems so known as my hand,
your flesh, the nakedness that makes them one, their being in
the wind impossible to say, nothing moving in our mouths
but that music that we saw within the wind. When you spoke,
I heard summer pass, the moon, then, a rose within your mouth.

Message

You came to say that fall was in the air, the eloquence that lay
upon the grass beneath the summer sun was gone, the silence now
diffused. I thought of crows when I was first awake, their black shapes
within the tree, the silence of the morning broken by their calls,
the tree, the grass and somewhere the sun covered by the sound. When we
no longer move within this life, echoes of us will within the air

resound, crows forever wakeful at their task. And so, then,
our spirits rose within the air, the fall filling us, nor could
I say who it was who heard, and what, but they were bones that sang
within the air, yours and mine, the grass inhaling us, the air
of its refracted breathing green, given ghostly to the sun,
crows in their processions over fields, a resonance of wings.

astoral

There is the morning's ripe fruit, hanging from the sky—: it glows,
no other autumn fruit possessing such dimension. The bees have done
their work, disappearing into light, all the rains, that might
have fallen, fell. Looking at you, the wonder of the sky within
your eyes, no one could distinguish bees from rain, the silence of
their leaving purgatories of the sense. How are we to bear

the tree of heaven so within, divine exemplar branching through
our flesh, bearing the light lately ripened, a dream of clarity
exhaled, investing us surprised in sudden nakedness, to wear
the transformation of the air, an innocence whose shape has no
knowing but the sense that we breathe, divinity the star
that rises in the heaven of our breath, Venus but a rose

transported in her hand? I touch your face, the sense of flesh
a light that grows within my hand, the bower of the sky a shade
that falls translucent on our skin. What kind of rose is this, to know
without nuance, no darkness that might appall the sun, the logic of
its rising the greater rose, the air unfolding us in its august
illuminings, an ancient garden taken shape against our feet?

*F*all

Above your head the sun within its autumn ripens, garnering
the light, and silence falling through the light. So eternities
in dream begin, a flower, rains of silence in the air, the sun
taking shape, and when you wake, seasons lie within your eyes,
birds coming back to settle there—the trees, the weathers and
the grass, the sun within its metamorphoses. I cannot think

of you as flesh. What have I, then, to touch, my fingers giving up
to silence and echoes of the silence entering your eyes?
The sun's fate is in your eyes, the fire unfolding the
inevitable rose, eternity exhaled without a sound.
I sit next to you. It is enough to breathe, a consonance
within the air, and music forever flowing over from your hands.

R

I see your hands were flowers in the dark. Their fragrance grew through
the room, rising into space, seeking the stars. The world has
no centre now, but somewhere under the sun and somewhere near
the flower of your hands the centre manifests itself to sense —:
what gravity is this, centripetal flower filling the mind, the laws
hanging in space, the planets in their dance becoming gardens that
the sun tends? What answer shall I give? Nothing that we say

can shape the fragrance there. Perhaps someday I shall awake to touch
flowers in the dark, their names unknown to me. Sentences
may come to mind, but so silent would their entrance be that I
should never find them in the dark. Give me, then, but one bloom
to take away, its darkness open, answering the sun. Your hands
are mortal too, fragilities that gesture somewhere knowing cannot
touch, beyond all waking where suns unfold their solitudes.

*T**aking Turn***

Backs against the sun we lay, surrendered wholly to the earth
turning through the air. If dying were a gesture, lying so
was our last oblation, autumn falling through us leaf by leaf,
infinite finalities of tree and grass entering our flesh.
I cannot tell you from the earth, nor you me, held within
our arms. Someday the sun will find us so, a fall of shades beneath
the trees, and birds within our shade will fly, suspended in

our gravity. We would not hear them sing, knowing but the air
and tremulous cadenzas shaping us. Whatever we become
it is the sun within that turns us so —bird, earth and tree —
a sun of no occasions but its own eternities. Apart
from this we cannot have epiphany, those tropics of
the soul and its material, earth forever in our breath,
and exhalations of the sun exchanged, transmuted in our mouth.

How can you be for me idea, a moon that rises in the mind,
trees and their shades upon the ground, a bird crying in the night,
a silence that pervades thought? When I take the simile
of your hand in mind, your flesh is where my brooding comes to rest,
adumbrations of your bones beneath. Where are you now, the ends
of your fingers meeting mine, if not forever reaching birth within
my eyes, auroras spilling through the air? I must be breathing you,

inhaling moons. Why speak, then, of bones, opacities
of flesh? Waking beside you in the dark, nothing is to hear
but tides against my back, a sound that rises on the shore, a moon
of music playing on my skin. Where within that fall of light,
that music overflowing, does my body end? This is how
eternities return to us, the shore of silence that we live within
falling down, a moon upon the sea, its fragments on the waves.

After rain the light unfolds the green ceremonies of
trees taking shape within your eyes. Where am I now to walk,
and where to breathe the exhalations of the earth, nothing that appears
that does not overflow—exemplars of the sun and planets—where
your gaze descends? What kind of immortality is this, to stand so
rapt in green? I think that I have died, nothing moving now

but light in metamorphosis, falling through fragilities
of flesh after rain. Necessity is not an ending, it
suffuses, outlines giving way. I cede all memory to you,
unable in the open garden of your eyes—the absolute
idea of green descending through their light—to know the trees, the sun
that falls, nor where whatever I have been has gone within the light.